Navigating ADHD:
Mindfulness, Time Management and Professional Development for Men with ADHD

By Dean M Chambers

TABLE OF CONTENTS

INTRODUCTION

What is ADHD and its effects on men?

ADHD, or Attention Deficit Hyperactivity Disorder, is a neurological condition that affects both children and adults. It is characterized by symptoms such as difficulty paying attention, impulsivity, and hyperactivity. These symptoms can make it hard for individuals with ADHD to focus on tasks, control their behaviour, and maintain relationships.

Men with ADHD often struggle with time management, organization, and planning. They may struggle to stay on task, complete projects, and have trouble regulating emotions. They may also struggle with social interactions and in professional settings. These difficulties can lead to feelings of frustration, anxiety, and low self-esteem.

Research suggests that men with ADHD may be more likely to engage in high-risk behaviours, such as substance abuse, and are more likely to have problems in their relationships and careers. They may also have higher rates of depression and anxiety.

It's important to note that ADHD is a highly individualized condition and each person's experience may differ. It's important to seek professional help and work with a healthcare professional to develop an appropriate treatment plan. With the right support, individuals with ADHD can manage their symptoms, improve their overall well-being and lead fulfilling lives.

As someone with ADHD, I have found that I have difficulty focusing on tasks, a tendency to talk excessively, and trouble waiting my turn in conversations and activities. I also have a tendency to act impulsively without fully considering the consequences. These symptoms are characteristic of ADHD and have affected my personal and professional life.

I understand the challenges of managing this disorder. I have found that incorporating certain exercises and techniques into my daily routine has helped me to improve my focus, reduce my symptoms, and overall improve my quality of life. I have compiled a series of chapters, each focusing on a different aspect of managing ADHD, and I would like to share them with you.

Purpose of the book

This activity book is designed specifically for men with ADHD to help them manage their symptoms and improve their overall well-being. Understanding that ADHD can make it hard for people to focus and control their actions, this book is filled with different activities, exercises and strategies that can help. Each chapter of the book begins with a short story that you may relate to, highlighting the struggles and successes of individuals with ADHD, followed by exercises and activities that you can practice to help you better manage your symptoms.

The book covers various topics, such as mindfulness exercises like meditation and breathing techniques, which can help you focus and calm down, as well as tips on how to make it a regular practice. It also covers ways to manage time better, break down big projects into smaller tasks and use a planner or calendar to keep on top of things.

It also includes physical activities like yoga, running and weightlifting that can help you focus and channel your energy in a good way and creative outlets like drawing, painting, and writing that can help you express yourself. Additionally, it provides exercises and tips to help you better communicate and interact with others and advice on handling social situations.

The book also covers problem-solving and decision-making, providing activities and tips on making better decisions and solving problems. It also includes advice on handling the workplace and setting yourself up for career success.

Lastly, it covers mind mapping, a way to organize your thoughts and ideas, which can be especially helpful for planning and decision-making. It includes instructions and examples to show you how to do it.

Overall, this book is here to help you manage your ADHD and improve your overall well-being with tips, tricks, and activities you can practice. With the help of this book, you can take control of your ADHD and unlock your full potential.

MINDFULNESS

John had been experiencing difficulties with attention and impulsivity due to his ADHD. Despite trying various medications and therapies, he had yet to find a solution that worked for him. His therapist then introduced the idea of mindfulness, which focuses on being present and fully engaged in the present moment, as a tool for managing his symptoms.

John was skeptical at first, but decided to give it a try. He started with simple breathing exercises and guided meditations. At first, it was difficult for him to focus and stay present, but with time and practice, he began to notice a change. He found that he was able to focus better, and that he was less impulsive. He also noticed that he was less stressed and anxious.

John's therapist also gave him tips and tricks for incorporating mindfulness into his daily life. He started to take regular breaks during the day to practice breathing exercises and meditation. He also found that he was more aware of his thoughts and emotions, which allowed him to respond to them in a more calm and thoughtful way.

John's mindfulness practice became a regular part of his daily routine. He noticed improvements in his focus and attention, his impulsivity and hyperactivity, and a decrease in stress and anxiety. Additionally, mindfulness helped him improve his relationships, career, and overall quality of life. He felt more in control of his ADHD than ever before and was able to live a fulfilling life.

John's story is an example of how mindfulness can be powerful tool for individuals with ADHD. Regular practice of mindfulness exercises can lead to improvements in symptoms and overall well-being. It's important to remember that it takes time and practice to establish a daily routine, but the benefits are worth it.

Guided Meditations

Body Scan Meditation: Start by finding a quiet place to sit or lie down. Close your eyes and focus on your breath. Slowly scan your body, starting at the top of your head and working your way down to your toes. Notice any tension or discomfort, and imagine breathing into those areas to release the tension. Continue to focus on your breath and scan your body for a few minutes.

Loving-Kindness Meditation: Begin by sitting comfortably and closing your eyes. Bring to mind someone you love and repeat the phrase, "may you be happy, may you be healthy, may you be safe, may you be at ease." Imagine sending them love and positive energy. Next, remember someone you are neutral towards and repeat the phrase for them. Finally, bring to mind someone you are in conflict with and repeat the phrase for them. Continue to repeat the phrase for yourself and for all beings.

Mindful Walking: Go for a walk in a quiet place and focus on the sensation of your feet hitting the ground. Notice the sensation of the air on your skin, the sound of nature, and the colours and textures of your surroundings. Take deep breaths and continue to focus on the present moment.

Breathing Exercises

4-7-8 Breathing: Inhale for 4 counts, hold for 7 counts, and exhale for 8 counts. Repeat for several minutes.

Box Breathing: Inhale for 4 counts, hold for 4 counts, exhale for 4 counts, hold for 4 counts. Repeat for several minutes.

Alternate Nostril Breathing: Close your right nostril with your thumb and inhale through your left nostril. Close your left nostril with your ring finger and exhale through your right nostril. Inhale through your right nostril, close it with your thumb, and exhale through your left nostril. Repeat for several minutes.

Mindfulness Tips and Tricks

Start small: If you're new to mindfulness, start with just a few minutes of meditation or breathing exercises each day. You can gradually increase the amount of time as you become more comfortable.

Make it a habit: Try to make mindfulness a regular part of your daily routine. This can help make it a consistent habit.

Find a comfortable place: Find a place where you feel comfortable and won't be disturbed during your mindfulness practice.

Use an app: Many mindfulness apps can guide you through meditation and breathing exercises. Experiment with a few to find one that works for you.

Be kind to yourself: Remember that mindfulness takes practice, so be patient with yourself and don't get discouraged if you find it difficult to focus or if your mind wanders during meditation.

Incorporate mindfulness into your daily activities: Try to bring mindfulness into your daily activities, such as washing the dishes or taking a shower. Focus on the sensation of the water on your skin and the smell of the soap.

Connect with nature: Mindfulness can be enhanced when practiced in nature. Try going for a walk in a park or near a lake or river and focus on your breath and the surroundings.

These are just a few examples of mindfulness exercises and tips that can be included in the activity book. It's important to note that mindfulness practice may require some experimentation to find the best fit for an individual. It's important to be patient with oneself and to remember that it takes time to establish a regular mindfulness practice.

1. How did you find this chapter?
2. Were the strategies provided in this chapter helpful for managing your symptoms?
3. How have you incorporated the techniques discussed in this chapter into your daily routine?
4. Have you noticed any improvements in your symptoms or overall well-being since incorporating these techniques?
5. Are there any additional strategies or techniques that you would like to see covered in future chapters?

_____

_____

_____

_____

_____

_____

_____

_____

TIME MANAGEMENT

Mike had always struggled with time management. He was easily distracted and found it hard to stay on task, often procrastinating until the last minute to complete projects. As a result, he was always stressed and behind schedule. He had tried different methods, but nothing seemed to work. One day, his therapist suggested that he try some time management strategies specifically designed for people with ADHD.

Mike was skeptical at first but decided to give it a try. He started with small changes, like breaking down larger projects into smaller tasks and using a planner to keep track of his schedule. He also tried to avoid procrastination by setting specific deadlines for himself. At first, it was difficult for him to stick to these new habits, but with time and practice, he began to notice a change.

He found that he was able to focus better and that he was less stressed. He also noticed that he was more organized and on top of things. He was able to complete tasks more efficiently and with less stress. He started to see improvements in his relationships, career, and overall quality of life.

Mike's story is an example of how time management strategies can be powerful tools for individuals with ADHD. Regular practice of time management strategies can lead to improvements in focus and attention and a decrease in stress and anxiety. Additionally, time management can help individuals with ADHD improve their relationships, career, and overall quality of life. It's important to remember that it takes time and practice to establish a daily routine, but the benefits are worth it.

Strategies for staying organized

To-do lists: Create a to-do list for each day or for the week. Prioritize the items on the list by importance and tackle them one by one. This will help you stay focused and on task and gives you a sense of accomplishment as you check items off the list.

Time blocking: Divide your day into blocks of time and assign specific tasks to each block. For example, you can dedicate the first hour of your day to checking emails and the next hour to working on a specific project. This will help you stay on track and avoid distractions.

Use a planner or calendar: Use a planner or calendar to schedule your tasks and deadlines. This will help you stay on top of important dates and events, and it will also help you prioritize your tasks.

Tips for breaking down larger projects

You can start with a goal: Before you begin a larger project, clearly define your goal and what you want to achieve. This will help you stay focused and on track as you work on the project.

Break it down: Break the larger project into smaller, manageable tasks. This will make the project more manageable and make it easier for you to track your progress.

Prioritize: Prioritize the smaller tasks by importance and tackle them one by one. This will help you stay focused and on track.

Strategies for avoiding procrastination

Use a timer: Set a timer for a specific amount of time, and work on a task for that amount of time. This will help you stay focused and on task, and it will also help you avoid procrastination.

Eliminate distractions from your work environment, such as social media notifications or unnecessary noise. This will help you stay focused and on task.

Get started: Sometimes, the hardest part of a task is getting started. Once you begin, you'll find it easier to keep going. So, if you're feeling stuck, start with something small, and then keep working on it.

These are just a few examples of the time management strategies and exercises that can be included in the activity book. It's important to note that time management skills may require some experimentation to find the best fit for an individual. It's important to be patient with oneself and to remember that it takes time to establish good time management habits.

1. How did you find this chapter?
2. Were the strategies provided in this chapter helpful for managing your symptoms?
3. How have you incorporated the techniques discussed in this chapter into your daily routine?
4. Have you noticed any improvements in your symptoms or overall well-being since incorporating these techniques?
5. Are there any additional strategies or techniques that you would like to see covered in future chapters?

_____

_____

_____

_____

_____

_____

_____

_____

PHYSICAL ACTIVITIES

Tom was dealing with the symptoms of ADHD, including difficulty focusing and an urge to constantly move. To help alleviate these symptoms, his therapist suggested incorporating regular physical activity into his daily routine. This would not only help him channel his energy in a positive way, but also improve his focus and reduce feelings of frustration and anxiety.

At first, Tom was hesitant. He had never been much of an athlete and wasn't sure he would enjoy it. But he was willing to give it a try. He started with yoga, as his therapist suggested it would be a good way to channel his energy in a positive way and help him focus better. He was surprised to find that he actually enjoyed it. He felt more focused and calm after his yoga sessions.

Encouraged by his success with yoga, Tom decided to try running. He found that the rhythmic motion of running helped him to focus better and reduce hyperactivity. He also started to lift weights, which helped him channel his energy in a positive way. He found that he enjoyed the feeling of accomplishment after a good workout.

Tom's story is an example of how physical activities can be powerful tools for individuals with ADHD. Regular exercise can help improve focus, reduce hyperactivity, and channel energy in a positive way. Additionally, regular exercise can improve overall well-being, such as better sleep, improved mood, and stronger physical health. By incorporating physical activities into their daily routine, men with ADHD can expect to see improvements in their symptoms and overall well-being.

Yoga

Warrior Pose: Stand with your feet hip-width apart and your arms extended out to the sides. Step your left foot back and bend your front knee, while keeping your back leg straight. Hold for 5-10 breaths, then switch sides. This pose can help improve focus and balance.

Downward-Facing Dog: Start on your hands and knees, with your wrists under your shoulders and your knees under your hips. Lift your hips up and back, straightening your arms and legs, so your body forms an inverted V shape. Hold for 5-10 breaths. This pose can help reduce stress and anxiety.

Child's Pose: Start on your hands and knees, with your wrists under your shoulders and your knees under your hips. Sit back on your heels and stretch your arms out in front of you. Lower your forehead to the floor and hold for 5-10 breaths. This pose can help relax the body and mind.

Running

Interval running: Start with a warm-up of a few minutes of jogging, then run at a high-intensity pace for 30 seconds, followed by 30 seconds of jogging. Repeat this interval for several minutes. This type of running can help improve focus and reduce hyperactivity.

Trail running: Find a nearby nature trail and go for a run. Changes in scenery and the natural environment can help improve focus and reduce stress.

Partner running: Find a running partner and go for a run together. Not only will this provide a sense of accountability, but it can also be a great way to socialize.

Weightlifting

Dumbbell press: Start by sitting on a bench with a dumbbell in each hand at shoulder level. Press the dumbbells up over your head, fully extending your arms. Lower the dumbbells back to shoulder level and repeat.

Pull-ups: Hang from a pull-up bar with your palms facing away from your body. Pull yourself up until your chin is over the bar. Lower yourself down and repeat.

Squats: Stand with your feet shoulder-width apart and your toes pointing forward. Lower your hips as if you were sitting back on a chair. Push through your heels to stand back up. Repeat.

Weightlifting can help improve focus and channel energy in a positive way.

These are just a few examples of physical activities that can be included in the activity book. It's important to note that physical activity may require some experimentation to find the best fit for an individual. it's important to start with a low-intensity workout and gradually increase the intensity as you become more comfortable. It's also important to consult with a doctor or a fitness professional before starting any new exercise

1. How did you find this chapter?
2. Were the strategies provided in this chapter helpful for managing your symptoms?
3. How have you incorporated the techniques discussed in this chapter into your daily routine?
4. Have you noticed any improvements in your symptoms or overall well-being since incorporating these techniques?
5. Are there any additional strategies or techniques that you would like to see covered in future chapters?

_____

_____

_____

_____

_____

_____

_____

CREATIVE OUTLETS

Ben, like many individuals with ADHD, found it difficult to focus and had a hard time sitting still. He often felt frustrated and anxious, not knowing how to channel his energy in a positive way. His therapist suggested that he try incorporating creative outlets into his daily routine to help manage his symptoms.

Ben wasn't sure what to expect, but he was willing to give it a try. He started withdrawing, as it seemed like a simple and easy place to begin. He found that he enjoyed the process of creating something with his hands. He felt more focused and calm while he was drawing. He also found that he enjoyed feeling accomplished when he was done with a drawing.

Encouraged by his success with drawing, Ben decided to try painting. He found that mixing colours and creating something with them helped him focus better and reduce stress. He also started to write, which helped him channel his energy in a positive way and express himself. He found that he enjoyed the feeling of accomplishment after writing.

Ben's story is an example of how creative outlets can be powerful tools for individuals with ADHD. Engaging in creative activities can help improve focus, reduce stress and anxiety, and improve overall well-being. Additionally, creative outlets can be a way for individuals with ADHD to express themselves and cope with their symptoms. By incorporating creative outlets into their daily routine, men with ADHD can expect to see improvements in their symptoms and overall well-being.

Drawing

Sketching: Grab a pencil and sketchbook and start drawing whatever comes to mind. It can be anything from objects to landscapes or even abstract shapes.

Drawing with a theme: Choose a theme, such as nature, cityscapes, or people, and draw based on that theme.

Drawing from photographs: Choose a photograph, and try to recreate it using pencils, markers, or other materials.

Drawing can help positively improve focus and channel energy.

Writing

Journaling: Start a journal and write down your thoughts, feelings, and experiences.

Creative writing: Write a short story or poem based on a prompt or an idea that you come up with.

Blogging: Start a blog and write about a topic that you're passionate about.

Writing can help positively improve focus and channel energy.

Painting

Abstract painting: Use acrylic or oil paint and paint whatever comes to mind.

Painting with a theme: Choose a theme, such as nature, cityscapes, or people, and paint based on that theme.

Painting from photographs: Choose a photograph and try to recreate it using acrylic or oil paint.

Painting can help positively improve focus and channel energy.

These are just a few examples of creative outlets that can be included in the activity book. It's important to remember that everyone has different interests and talents, so it's important to find an activity that resonates with you and that you enjoy doing. Also, it's important to remember that it's not about the final product but about the process of creating and expressing oneself. Engaging in creative activities can help individuals with ADHD focus, channel their energy positively and reduce stress and anxiety.

Other creative outlets for channeling energy include:

Music: Playing an instrument or singing can be a great way to channel energy and improve focus.

Dancing: Dancing can be a great form of exercise and a way to channel energy positively.

Acting: Acting in a play or a theatre group can be a great way to express oneself and positively channel energy.

Photography: Photography can be a great way to channel energy positively and capture and express beauty worldwide.

Cooking: Cooking can be a great way to channel energy positively and create delicious and nutritious meals.

Gardening: Gardening can be a great way to channel energy positively and connect with nature.

Pottery: Pottery can be a great way to channel energy positively and create something beautiful and functional with your hands.

Woodworking: Woodworking can be a great way to channel energy positively, and to create something beautiful and functional with your hands.

Sewing: Sewing can be a great way to positively channel energy and create something beautiful and functional with your hands.

Sculpture: Sculpture can be a great way to positively channel energy and create something beautiful and meaningful with your hands.

These are just a few examples of creative outlets that can be used to channel energy positively. Finding an activity that resonates with you and that you enjoy doing is important. Remember that it's not about the final product, but about the process of creating and expressing oneself.

1. How did you find this chapter?
2. Were the strategies provided in this chapter helpful for managing your symptoms?
3. How have you incorporated the techniques discussed in this chapter into your daily routine?
4. Have you noticed any improvements in your symptoms or overall well-being since incorporating these techniques?
5. Are there any additional strategies or techniques that you would like to see covered in future chapters?

_____

_____

_____

_____

_____

_____

_____

SOCIAL SKILLS

Robert had always been a bit of a loner. He didn't have many friends and often felt isolated in social situations. But when he was diagnosed with ADHD, he realized that some of his struggles with socializing resulted from his condition. He was determined to improve his social skills and turned to the chapter on social skills training in his activity book for men with ADHD.

The first technique he tried was active listening. He practiced really focusing on the person he was talking to and trying to understand what they were saying. He noticed that this helped him to feel more engaged in conversations and less anxious. He also learned effective communication techniques, such as how to express himself clearly and ask questions. This helped him to have more meaningful conversations with people.

Robert also worked on understanding nonverbal cues. He learned how to read body language and facial expressions, which helped him to understand how others were feeling and respond accordingly. He practiced these techniques in different social situations, such as at work and with friends.

As Robert continued to work on improving his social skills, he noticed a significant improvement in his relationships. He felt more comfortable in social situations and could easily connect with others. He also felt more confident in his ability to communicate and understand others. Improving his social skills also helped him in his professional life as he built better relationships with his colleagues and clients. Robert was happy to find that he could improve his overall well-being by working on his social skills.

Communication Exercises

Role-playing: Practice different scenarios such as making a complaint or asking for help, with a partner or in a group setting. This will help you to develop your communication skills and become more confident in real-life situations.

Reflective listening: Practice reflecting back on what the other person has said and paraphrasing it in your own words. This will help improve your listening skills and ensure that you understand the other person's message correctly.

Nonverbal communication: Practice different nonverbal communication techniques such as maintaining eye contact and using appropriate body language and tone of voice. This will help you to convey your message more effectively and understand the other person's message better.

Interpersonal Skills Tips

Self-awareness: Practice self-awareness and pay attention to your own behaviour and reactions. This will help you to understand how you come across to others and make any necessary adjustments.

Empathy: Try to put yourself in the other person's shoes and understand their perspective. This will help you to build stronger relationships and communicate more effectively.

Conflict Resolution: Learn techniques for resolving conflicts such as active listening and compromise. This will help you to navigate difficult social situations and maintain healthy relationships.

Navigating Social Situations

Small talk: Practice making small talk and conversing with people you meet. This will help you feel more comfortable in social situations and build connections.

Networking: Learn how to network effectively and make a good first impression in professional settings. This will help you to build connections and open up new opportunities.

Social etiquette: Learn about social etiquette and customs, such as how to introduce yourself, how to accept and decline invitations, and how to navigate group settings. This will help you to navigate social situations more confidently and comfortably.
It's important to remember that social skills training may require some experimentation to find the best fit for an individual and that it takes time to establish a daily routine. It's important to be patient with yourself and to remember that it's normal to have bad days, but with the help of these techniques, it's possible to improve social skills and overall well-being.

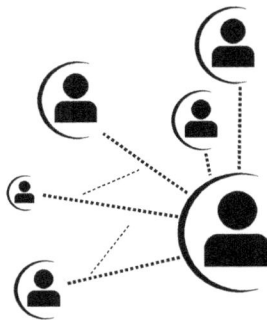

1. How did you find this chapter?
2. Were the strategies provided in this chapter helpful for managing your symptoms?
3. How have you incorporated the techniques discussed in this chapter into your daily routine?
4. Have you noticed any improvements in your symptoms or overall well-being since incorporating these techniques?
5. Are there any additional strategies or techniques that you would like to see covered in future chapters?

_____

_____

_____

_____

_____

_____

_____

PROBLEM-SOLVING AND DECISION-MAKING

Feeling frustrated with his inability to make progress in his personal and professional life, Paul decided to take action. He began researching different problem-solving and decision-making techniques that could help him navigate and solve challenges more effectively.

He learned about the importance of breaking down problems into smaller, manageable pieces, generating multiple options before making a decision, and evaluating each option before selecting the best course of action.

To put these techniques into practice, Paul started by creating a list of all the decisions he needed to make and the problems he needed to solve. He then worked on breaking each one down into smaller tasks that he could tackle one by one.

As he began to make progress, Paul started to feel more confident in his ability to solve problems and make decisions. He also noticed that his relationships with friends and family improved and his ability to manage his workload at work.

Paul realized that with the right techniques and a bit of practice, he could overcome his difficulties with problem-solving and decision-making. He was grateful for the newfound sense of control over his life and was excited to continue improving his skills.

Activities and exercises

Mind Mapping: Use a mind map to break down a problem into smaller parts. Draw a central idea and branch out with related ideas. This will help you to see the problem from different perspectives and identify potential solutions.

Brainstorming: Gather a group of people and generate as many ideas and options as possible to solve a problem. This will help you to think outside the box and come up with unique solutions.

Role-playing: Practice different scenarios in which you need to solve a problem or make a decision. This will help you to become more confident and comfortable in real-life situations.

Tips for Improving Decision-Making

Gather Information: Gather as much information as possible before making a decision; this will help you to make a more informed decision.

Consider the Consequences: Consider the potential consequences of each option before making a decision; this will help you to make a decision that is in your best interest.

Take your time: Take your time, and don't rush into a decision. This will help you to avoid impulsive decisions and make sure that you have considered all of your options.

Strategies for Solving Problems

Root Cause Analysis: Identify the root cause of a problem; this will help you to find a more effective solution.

The 5 Whys: Ask "why" five times to understand the cause of a problem; this will help you to identify the root cause and find a solution.

SWOT Analysis: Analyze the strengths, weaknesses, opportunities, and threats of a problem; this will help you to find a solution that addresses all of the factors involved.

It's important to remember that problem-solving and decision-making may require some experimentation to find the best fit for an individual and that it takes time to establish a daily routine. It's important to be patient with yourself and to remember that it's normal to have bad days, but with the help of these techniques, it's possible to improve problem-solving and decision-making skills and overall well-being.

1. How did you find this chapter?
2. Were the strategies provided in this chapter helpful for managing your symptoms?
3. How have you incorporated the techniques discussed in this chapter into your daily routine?
4. Have you noticed any improvements in your symptoms or overall well-being since incorporating these techniques?
5. Are there any additional strategies or techniques that you would like to see covered in future chapters?

_____

_____

_____

_____

_____

_____

_____

_____

PROFESSIONAL DEVELOPMENT

Matthew had always felt like he was at a disadvantage in the workplace due to his ADHD. He struggled with time management and organization, which often affected his performance and made it difficult for him to advance in his career. Despite his challenges, he was determined to succeed in his field and decided to take action.

He began by focusing on his professional development. He started networking with colleagues and industry professionals, building a strong professional brand, and developing a career plan. He took the time to understand his strengths and weaknesses and worked on developing strategies to overcome his challenges.

Through this process, Matthew found that he could improve his performance and began to see progress in his career. His networking led to new job opportunities, and he established himself as a valuable asset. He also found that having a clear career plan gave him a sense of direction and purpose, helping him to stay motivated and focused.

Matthew saw his career take off as he continued to work on his professional development. He was promoted to a higher position, received recognition for his work, and felt a sense of satisfaction and fulfillment in his job. He realized that by focusing on his professional development, he could overcome his ADHD challenges and succeed in his career.

Navigating the workplace

Identify strengths: Identify your strengths and how they can be applied in the workplace. This will help you to focus on what you are good at and how you can contribute to the organization.

Learn to manage distractions: Identify and manage distractions in the workplace such as social media, email, or phone notifications. This will help you to stay focused and be more productive.

Build relationships: Build relationships with colleagues, supervisors, and mentors. This will help you to establish a support system and open up new opportunities.

Setting oneself up for success in a career

Networking: Build a professional network by attending events, joining professional organizations, and connecting with colleagues and mentors. This will help you to build connections and open up new opportunities.

Personal branding: Create a personal brand by developing a professional image and online presence. This will help you to establish a positive reputation and stand out in the job market.

Career development plan: Create a career development plan that outlines your long-term career goals and the steps you need to take to achieve them. This will help you to stay focused and motivated.

Strategies for career advancement

Continual learning: Continuously learn new skills and knowledge to stay current in your field and increase your value to the organization.

Seek out leadership opportunities: Seek out leadership opportunities such as mentoring, volunteering for projects, or leading teams. This will help you to develop leadership skills and increase visibility within the organization.

Look for opportunities: Be proactive and look for opportunities to advance your career, such as job openings, promotions, or stretch assignments.

It's important to remember that professional development may require some experimentation to find the best fit for an individual and that it takes time to establish a daily routine. It's important to be patient with yourself and to remember that it's normal to have bad days. Still, with the help of these techniques, it's possible to improve professional development and overall well-being.

1. How did you find this chapter?
2. Were the strategies provided in this chapter helpful for managing your symptoms?
3. How have you incorporated the techniques discussed in this chapter into your daily routine?
4. Have you noticed any improvements in your symptoms or overall well-being since incorporating these techniques?
5. Are there any additional strategies or techniques that you would like to see covered in future chapters?

_____

_____

_____

_____

_____

_____

_____

_____

MIND MAPPING

Nicholas had always needed help to stay organized and on task. As someone with ADHD, he often struggled with managing his thoughts and completing projects. That is until he discovered mind mapping.

Mind mapping is a technique that allows individuals to organize their thoughts and ideas visually using diagrams, symbols, and colours. Nicholas learned how to create a mind map by breaking down a big project into smaller tasks and connecting them with lines and arrows. He also discovered the importance of visual aids, such as images and colours, to help him better understand and remember the information.

By incorporating mind mapping into his daily routine, Nicholas noticed a significant improvement in his ability to stay organized and on task. He could break down complex information, generate new ideas, and remember important details. Mind mapping also helped him to plan better and make better decisions. It was a valuable tool that improved not only his productivity but also his overall well-being.

Instructions and Examples

Creating a Mind Map: Start with a central idea or topic, and branch out with related ideas. Use lines and arrows to connect related ideas and create a visual representation of the information.

Brainstorming: Use a mind map to brainstorm and generate new ideas. This will help you to think creatively and come up with unique solutions.

Note-taking: Use a mind map to take notes and organize information. This will help you to stay focused and understand complex information.

Using mind mapping for planning and decision-making

Setting goals: Use a mind map to set and organize specific, measurable, achievable, relevant, and time-bound goals (SMART Goals)

Prioritizing: Use a mind map to prioritize tasks and goals based on their importance and urgency.

Decision-making: Use a mind map to analyze a problem, generate options, and evaluate and select the best course of action.

1. How did you find this chapter?
2. Were the strategies provided in this chapter helpful for managing your symptoms?
3. How have you incorporated the techniques discussed in this chapter into your daily routine?
4. Have you noticed any improvements in your symptoms or overall well-being since incorporating these techniques?
5. Are there any additional strategies or techniques that you would like to see covered in future chapters?

_____

_____

_____

_____

_____

_____

_____

_____

CONCLUSION

In this book, we have discussed various strategies and techniques that can help men with ADHD to improve their overall well-being. From mindfulness and relaxation techniques to time management and professional development, each chapter has provided practical tools and exercises that can be incorporated into daily life.

It's important to remember that each individual with ADHD is unique and may require different strategies and techniques to manage their symptoms. It's important to be patient with yourself and to remember that it's normal to have bad days. It takes time to establish a daily routine and finding what works best for you is important.

It's also important to remember that ADHD is a lifelong condition, and it's important to continue to work on managing symptoms throughout adulthood. With the help of the techniques provided in this book, individuals with ADHD can improve their overall well-being and live a fulfilling life.

I hope that this book has provided you with valuable information and tools that you can use to improve your overall well-being. I would like to encourage you to continue to explore different strategies and techniques and to work with your healthcare provider to find the best approach for you. Remember that you are not alone and that you can manage your symptoms and live a fulfilling life with the right support and resources.

Summary of key takeaways

1. ADHD is a lifelong condition that requires ongoing management.
2. Different techniques and strategies may work better for some individuals than others.
3. Mindfulness and relaxation techniques can help to improve symptoms such as impulsivity and hyperactivity.
4. Time management and professional development techniques can help to improve performance and career advancement.
5. Mind mapping can be useful for organizing thoughts, breaking down complex information, and generating new ideas.
6. it's important to work with a healthcare provider to find the best approach for managing symptoms.
7. With the right support and resources, individuals with ADHD can manage their symptoms and live a fulfilling life.

Additional resources for men with ADHD

CHADD (Children and Adults with Attention-Deficit/Hyperactivity Disorder) - https://www.chadd.org/
ADDitude Magazine - https://www.additudemag.com/category/adhd-adult/
ADHD Coach Academy - https://www.adhdcoachacademy.com/
ADHD Men's Support Group - https://www.facebook.com/groups/ADHDmen/
ADHD Roller Coaster - https://www.adhdrollercoaster.org/
Adult ADHD Information - https://www.helpguide.org/articles/add-adhd/adult-adhd-attention-deficit-disorder.htm
ADDitude Resource Center - https://www.additudemag.com/resource-center-adhd-adult/
ADHD Professional Resource - https://www.adhdprofessional.com/
ADHD in Adult - https://www.helpguide.org/articles/add-adhd/adult-adhd-attention-deficit-disorder.htm
WebMD ADHD Health Center - https://www.webmd.com/add-adhd/default.htm

It's important to note that some resources may not be reliable or up-to-date, and it's always good to consult a healthcare professional before making any changes in treatment or lifestyle.

I invite you to join my mailing list to stay up to date on new releases and other resources that can help you on your journey. Simply scan the QR code below to sign up and stay connected. Thank you for reading and best of luck on your journey to success.

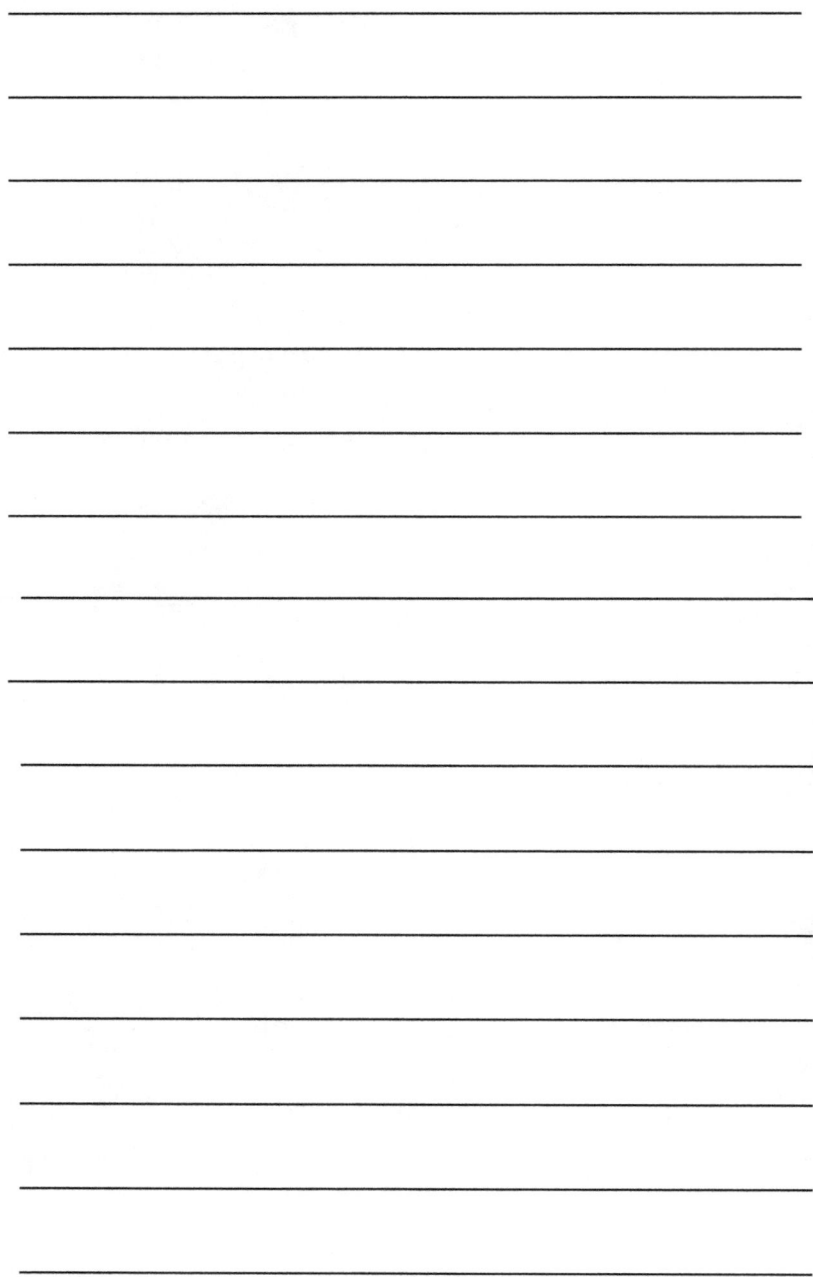

www.ingramcontent.com/pod-product-compliance
Lightning Source LLC
Chambersburg PA
CBHW030030290326
41934CB00005B/561